HOW TO FIND YOURSELF WHEREVER YOU ARE

AMBER CHAISSON

PUBLISHED BY

Printed in the United States of America

First Printing, 2017

ISBN:978-0-9916015-7-8

Copyright © 2016 Amber Chaisson

All rights reserved. No part of this publication may be reproduced, distributed, or transmitted in any form or by any means, including photocopying, recording, or other electronic or mechanical methods, without the prior written permission of the publisher, except in the case of brief quotations embodied in critical reviews and certain other noncommercial uses permitted by copyright law. For permission requests, write to the publisher, addressed "Attention: Permissions Coordinator," at the address below.

13th & Joan

500 N. Michigan Avenue, Suite #500

Chicago, il 60611

www.13thandjoan.com

DEDICATION

STRENGTH
I dedicate this book to Ramona, my mother. Thank you for giving me life and guiding me through the highest and lowest points of my life. Your strength will resonate in my heart forever.

LOVE
I dedicate this book to Gerard, my father. You taught me about love and I will write many chapters of my life with my heart forever.

LIFE
I dedicate this book to Ojo, my spiritual father. You helped me to achieve my dreams in ways that I could never imagine. My gratitude towards you will live eternally.

FRIENDSHIP
I dedicate this book to all of my friends, family and supporters. I am beyond thankful for your love and kindness towards me.

- From the Pen of Ace

CONTENTS

INTRODUCTION: DEPARTURE

CH. 1: FAITH

CH. 2: CONFIDENCE

CH. 3: SELF ESTEEM

CH. 4: AFFIRMATION

CH. 5: APPRECIATION

CH. 6: TRUST

CH. 7: FREEDOM

CONCLUSION: ARRIVAL

INTRODUCTION

So here you are, going day to day existing and never stopping to take the time to live. It is possible that you are unsatisfied with what and who you see when you look in the mirror. It is possible that you don't know who you are at all.

With over 7 billion people in the world, it is possible that you feel alone, confused and a bit misunderstood. Or perhaps you are not content with where you are in your life, and seek to uncover more of yourself. And as much as you may feel alone, know that you are not. I repeat, you are not alone.

In fact, every human on earth feels the way you do at some point in their lives. The goal then becomes to navigate through these challenges and build your inner and outer shields of armor.

How you deal with the deeply rooted emotions of your inner being is what defines who you become as you journey through life.

These same guiding principles dictate how you interact with and journey through the lives of others.
No matter what happens, you must discover true happiness. To this end, your happiness must not be dependent on any one person nor tangible, material or monetary factors. Your truest self is where happiness must be discovered.

I wrote this book to help you navigate the journey towards happiness wherever you are right now, in your life and in this world.

This piece of work is personal to me because like you, I too find myself lost in the dark trenches of life from time to time. I'm certain that you can agree that life is not about where you begin, but where you end is all that truly matters.

Journey with me.

> A FLOWER DOES NOT BLOSSOM BECAUSE IT THINKS IT CAN. IT KNOWS IT CAN, AND SO IT DOES.

— ACE

When you were created, you were not created with the spirit of fear. When a seed is planted, it blossoms and grows into a flower, because that is what it is supposed to do. It does not doubt or fear it's transition.

The same principle applies to you. You are a creature of learned habits. You practice what you have learned, and apply it in all areas of your life. This includes fear. You often inhibit yourself because of what you think can hold you back, when in reality you are often the only roadblock.
Let that fear go! It is not real.

Whatever it is that is holding you back, is not real. It is an illusion that you have to not only recognize but also see past in order to realize your blossoming moment. Keep going, keep fighting, keep pushing. And when you think you can't, remember that you are fighting the same battle as many others.
You are not alone.

Look so deeply inside of yourself that you know exactly what you want, and then go for it. When you look up, you'll have exactly what you've always wanted. Set yourself free and watch your happiness grow. The only requirement is faith. When you believe that you can, you can. And the most beautiful part is that you will.

> IT ALL STARTS WITH HAVING FAITH IN YOURSELF, EVEN WHEN NO ONE ELSE DOES.

– ACE

As they always say, seeing is believing, but many times you doubt what you can do until you have proven it to others. Often times you find yourself allowing doubt to put the things you believe in,
last instead of first.

It is inevitable to fight this human instinct, but the power of belief and faith can erase any doubt or unseen thing. Face your fears with faith. Know that whatever it is that you are trying to achieve starts with you. Plunge head first into your dreams.

Many times you will find yourself walking into your destiny alone. The road will be long and your path will be unmarked, but having faith within yourself will be the light at the end of your tunnel.

You may feel like you are at the bottom of your barrel. This is always how it feels right before the greatest moments of our lives. Trust what is meant for you no matter what you are striving for.

> BELIEF IS LIKE LOVE. IT IS A FEELING DEEP INSIDE OF YOU THAT YOU HAVE TO TRUST WITH ALL OF YOUR HEART, MIND, BODY AND SOUL.

— ACE

Beautiful things happen when you trust your faith. It's almost like a magic that's around you when you believe in yourself. People can see the magic, people can see your glow, the beauty in your confidence and when you believe in yourself.

There is nothing like trusting what is inside of you, and the fuel that drives you. When you believe in yourself others will believe in you. No matter what you are striving for, you must believe with all of your heart. There may be someone somewhere in the world that is influenced by your strength.

Do not let doubts, fears, and lack of confidence from others drain your magic. When you wake up everyday, wake up with a resilience that can't be broken. Believe, believe, believe and believe some more!

Don't doubt yourself, only believe. Keep going, keep fighting, and keep believing.

"

STEPPING OUT ON YOUR FAITH IS THE BEST FEELING IN THE WORLD. KNOWING THAT YOU WON'T FALL IS EVEN BETTER.

– ACE

Have you ever tried to drive a car with no gas? Have you ever tried to eat in the absence of food? Chances are, your answer is no. Have you ever gone through life not believing in yourself? We all have.

You must recognize that you have been called to dig deeper. Whatever it is that you are seeking to achieve, you must be willing to step out on the sheer belief that whatever you set your heart, mind, and goals towards, will bear success.

Faith in yourself is the key to unlocking true happiness. Talk yourself into trying new things, speaking with different people, and challenging yourself everyday to do something you have never done before. This liberation exudes the ultimate confidence.

When you believe that anything is possible, anything can happen. Be a soldier for your faith. Be the strongest believer in yourself. Set yourself up for success, and set a standard that will enforce others to do the same.

Trust that if anything goes wrong you can always chart a new course along the way.

"

POUR OUT YOUR FEARS
AND FILL YOUR HEART
WITH FAITH.

- ACE

Time and time again, I have seen the damaging effects that fear can have on a person's life. It often appears to place a choke hold on dreams and aspirations Fear really doesn't exist. Why allow something that doesn't exist to stifle the growth in your life?

When you pour out all of the fears that you create in your mind, your heart can be free. You must eliminate distractions, ignore doubts, and triumph over defeat to reach victory. The life you want is possible when you believe it enough to bring it to fruition.

Nothing can happen until you push your fears aside. Close your eyes, and become a force that can break any wall blocking you from your destiny.

Continue to fight for what you believe in, until the things that you believe in, fight for you.

"

BELIEVE IN YOUR CRAZY DREAMS. FIGHT FOR THE THINGS THAT MAKES YOU HAPPY. BE A BELIEVER OF YOU.

- ACE

No matter how crazy, stupid, or strange your dreams may be to someone else, remember that one day you can change the face of a nation. Be bold in what you believe in.

Do not cater your dreams and what it is that you are fighting for most, towards making the generation of today happy. Dig deep within yourself and fight for what truly makes your heart beat.

Life isn't supposed to make sense all the time. Life is meant for you to make mistakes and experience failures and heartaches as you journey towards your rainbow. Know that is lies at the end of the storm.

The beauty in the madness is that you are here to live your best life possible and you do so by being exactly who you are and knowing that what is meant for you is truly for you.

No matter how many obstacles you have to face to get to you reward in life, it all belongs to you. The moral of this story is, believe, fight, and achieve for yourself.

"

GO TO WAR FOR YOUR DREAMS. BE A SOLDIER FOR YOUR HEART. GUARD WHAT YOU LOVE WITH EVERYTHING THAT YOU HAVE. AND KNOW THAT YOUR FAITHFULNESS DOES NOT GO UNNOTICED.

- ACE

You have to fight for what you love. There is no better feeling in the world than to protect, and guard the things that you love, knowing that it will pay off in the end.

You must be a warrior for the things that you aspire to achieve.. Nothing comes easy, but when you are persistent in your goals, the things that you dream about will come to fruition.

The same goes for the things that you love. Have faith in your dreams and the people that you love. What you put out will always come back to you, including love, faith, and protection.

> "

USE THE OPINIONS, DOUBTS, AND REJECTION OF OTHERS TO FUEL YOUR ENGINE. IT WILL TAKE YOU FURTHER THAN ANY OTHER FUEL YOU'VE EVER USED. LET IT BE THE FUEL OF YOUR LIFE.

— ACE

Many times in life you face obstacles. These obstacles usually come in the form of others who doubt you. Every single day of your life, there will be challenges that you must overcome. You have to focus on using these obstacles as fuel.

Whether you experience pressure from peers, social media, colleagues, or even love, you must know how to use these pressures to reveal your inner diamond. When you learn how to use the rejection of others as your own personal fuel, you will find that it is unlike any other fuel you've ever used.

The opinions doubts, and rejection of others will allow you to discover your power. The key is to not let rejection break you. Let it build you higher and higher, until you find yourself elevated above the factors that never mattered to begin with.

This is your life, live it according to your own terms and conditions.

> FEAR IS ONLY A WEED IN YOUR LIFE. REMOVE IT AND REPLACE IT WITH SEEDS OF FAITH. WATER THEM WITH BELIEF. AND WATCH CONFIDENCE, HAPPINESS, AND PURPOSE GROW.

– ACE

The only time that something can grow is when it is fed. The same principle applies to the spirit of fear. If you view fear as a weed, then you can also view it as something that can easily be removed.

Sometimes the biggest obstacles in our lives, are only obstacles because we allow them to be. When fear is replaced with faith, magic happens. You have to dig deep into the pit of your soul, and believe that confidence, happiness, and positivity all starts with you.

There is nothing like allowing something that doesn't exist to block you. Set yourself free and grow on purpose.

> FIGHT. PUSH. PULL. KICK. AND SCREAM FOR WHAT YOU BELIEVE IN. THE ONLY REQUIREMENT IS BELIEVING.

– ACE

When a baby cries for milk, when children fight for a toy, or when a dog growls for a bone, it is because they all want something they believe belongs to them. They have no doubt that it belongs to anyone else besides themselves.

The same goes for you. You have to fight, push, pull, kick, and even scream for what you believe in. The key word is "believe".

Often times your thoughts are the main factors in what becomes of you life. What you believe in is a direct dictates where your journey will end. Push your mind, body, and soul to the limits.

Your thoughts are your destiny, and your destiny is already yours if you just believe that it is. Nothing can stop you, not even you.

CHAPTER 2
SELF-COURAGE is CONFIDENCE

> BE SO COURAGEOUS THAT YOU SHOCK YOURSELF IN THE PROCESS.

- ACE

Learning how to build courage is a process. It takes time to cultivate your seed of courage. This seed will grow and become a defining factor in your life, as you navigate through the highs and lows of your journey.

This same journey will take you through some of the greatest times, and some of the worst times. There will be times that will make you happy and times that will make you doubt everything.

Having the courage to step out of your comfort zone and take on life is what will shift your circumstances towards an entirely new level.

Have faith, have confidence and have courage to go for it. Don't doubt yourself. Be so bold and courageous in your actions that you shock yourself in the process.

> HAVE THE AUDACITY TO LIVE FEARLESSLY. YOU'LL NEVER REGRET IT.

— ACE

Can you imagine living life without fear? What if fear did not exist? I am here to tell you that it doesn't! Do not allow things that do not exist to control you.

Be audacious, be daring, be willing to step up on the stage of your world and live without fear. What is the worst that can come from living a life that is not inhibited by fear? The answer is nothing!

In fact, when you dismiss all doubts, holds, and fears over your life, you will learn that living fearlessly will leave you with no regrets.

Find new ways to challenge your limits and push yourself as far, as open, and as wide as you possibly can! You'll thank yourself forever.

> I USED TO CONFUSE COURAGE WITH CRAZINESS UNTIL I BECAME COURAGEOUS.

– ACE

Many times, people view those who are courageous as crazy. The ones who are fearless, daring, and brave are often times misinterpreted and as a result, misunderstood. I was this same person.

The one who was too timid to speak up or stand up for myself, and as a result, I envied those who were bold enough to do just that. I saw these people as crazy, loud, and outspoken, never taking the time to understand why they were so confident, and where their confidence came from.

Until I became that person myself. I had to go through the ringers of life to get to a point where I had no choice but to stand up for myself and be courageous in all that I stood for. I am still standing and I am here to tell you that you can do the same.

Be so courageous that you influence and inspire someone the way that others inspire you. Be the difference, the reason, and the light. It always shines through.

> KNOW THAT YOUR ENDURANCE WILL NOT GO IN VAIN. YOU ARE A VICTOR, NOT A VICTIM.

– ACE

Everyday that you wake up, you may encounter obstacles. These obstacles may be gradual, or they may arrive all at once. We all have hurdles to jump over, but as long as we keep in mind that these hurdles can always be overcome, as long as we are alive.

The more pain you endure in your life, the greater your reward will be. We all face challenges in our lives, and while some are harder than others, the key is not what you face, but how you face it.

Always remember that your endurance through the hard times will not go in vain. Know that you are not a victim, you are a victor.

> WITH FORTITUDE ON YOUR SIDE, IT IS HARD TO FAIL. WITH COURAGE IN YOUR HEART, IT IS HARD TO CAVE.

— ACE

I believe that everything in life is dependent heavily on fortitude. There is a certain amount of resilience you were born with when you came into this world.

You must tap into this fortitude and resilience as you transition into different phases of your life, in order to fight the spirit of failure or defeat that has a tendency to creep into your path from time to time.

As long as you remember that you are built with the fortitude and willpower to face anything that is thrown your way, it will be nearly impossible for you to fail.

Keep your strength, and let it be the light that allows you to shine through your darkest times.

> BE FOREVER RELENTLESS IN YOUR PURSUIT OF FINDING THE STRONGEST PERSON YOU KNOW. YOURSELF.

— ACE

What if I told you that you are the strongest person you will ever meet? Would you believe me?
This is a fact.

Every day that you wake up, every glance you take in the mirror, every challenge you overcome, and every breath you take makes you the greatest person in your life. You may come across people who inspire you, motivate you, and even influence you, but the key word is YOU.

What you see in others and in the world is only a reflection of what is inside of you. You attract what and who you are. Be the power you see. Feel the love you feel. Breed the positivity you receive.

You are the champion of your life at all times. Know it, and own it!

> IF WE STARTED OUT KNOWING WHO WE WERE GOING TO BE, WE MIGHT NOT FIND THE STRENGTH IN THE PROCESS TO BECOME THAT PERSON.

- ACE

If you could see yourself five, ten, or even twenty years from now, who would you want to see? Who would you want to be? If you were the person you were destined to be years from now, right now, what growth would you have experienced? The answer is none.

You have to push yourself every day to build a better, stronger, fiercer version of yourself, so that in the years to come, you will thank the old you for the fight.

Invest time towards doing what makes you happy, and ultimately this will lead you into your destiny, and your happiness.

Focus on the things that are a true reflection of you, and indulge in your truth. In the process of your building, you will look back and forever thank yourself for leaving room to grow into the best version of you.

> IT TAKES THE SPIRIT OF A KING, TO HAVE THE HUMILITY OF A NOBLE, THE GRACE OF A QUEEN, AND THE COURAGE OF A KNIGHT.

— ACE

Embrace taking on different sides of yourself. Be open to learning yourself like you've never done before.

Know what makes you happy, know what hurts you, and know what can bring the best out of you. You possess the qualities of everyone and everything that touches the core of you.

You can enjoy the pleasures of a king, but you must also recognize the pain of a peasant. Humble yourself in order to relate to others, and in return you will be elevated.

> IT TAKES COURAGE TO GET YOU IN THE ROOM, IT TAKES CONFIDENCE TO STAY THERE.

— ACE

Some say it's charm, others say it's charisma. Very few realize that it's courage which can make room for you.

Having the bravery to stand firm in what you believe in can take you as far as you want it to. This is true power. Take this power, harness it and nurture it so that it can benefit you in the best ways of your life.

Know that your courage may place you amongst others as great as yourself, or greater, but your confidence is what will hold you amongst these ranks. Never lose sight of what you are working towards.

Lift yourself above the rest by staying grounded in confidence, and simply believing that you are capable of anything.

"

THE SAME INTESTINAL FORTITUDE THAT LIES WITHIN YOUR HEROES, LIES WITHIN YOU. YOU CAN ONLY SEE WHAT YOU ARE A REFLECTION OF.

- ACE

You look up to your idols, influencers, and heroes because you see yourself in them. There is a subconscious that forces you to gravitate towards those who you can relate to.

The only difference between you and your heroes is timing. Use what your influences have taught you, build on it, and be much better.

Focus on the best parts of yourself and tap so deep into it, that you get lost in your greatness. Then come out of your trenches, and rise like a Phoenix.

Rise up as your own hero, and know that the same intestinal fortitude that lies within your heroes, lies right inside of you.

CHAPTER 3
SELF-RESPECT is ESTEEM

"

RESPECT IS A GIVEN.
ALTHOUGH IT IS
NOT ALWAYS GIVEN.
DEMAND IT, DON'T
DISMISS IT.

- ACE

Respect should not be something that we are passive about. Respect should be a given. If you are going through your life without demanding respect, how will it ever be given to you?

As you progress through the many phases of life, you come to realize that respect is everything. You begin to learn that people don't have to like you, but they have to respect you.

If they can't respect you, more than likely they can't do anything for you. When you respect yourself, others around you will have no choice but to do the same.

Demand respect, don't dismiss it.
After all, you deserve it.

> SELF-RESPECT IS LIKE EATING. IT'S NECESSARY IN ORDER TO HAVE A HEALTHY LIFE.

— ACE

Self respect is key. If you feel as though you are at a point where you are not receiving the respect you feel as though you deserve, you may need to reevaluate how you view yourself.

You can only get what you give. You cannot expect anymore or any less. Self respect is like a key ingredient to a healthy, nutritious, thriving life. It starts with you.

It starts with everything that you believe you are. It starts as soon as you look in the mirror. It starts when you get dressed, and go out into the world.

Live with the respect you expect from others. It will only come back to you in the best possible way.

"

THERE IS ONLY ONE TYPE OF RESPECT. RESPECT.

- ACE

Respect is black and white. There is no grey. Many times people try to make excuses for the way they treat you, when in reality they are disguising a lack of respect.

When you understand that respect only comes in one form, you will know when to recognize it, and when to accept it.

And at the same time, when not to accept anything that is not respect. Place yourself at a higher standard, and the same regard from others will follow.

There are no secrets about this. Try it. Start now. Recognize respect when you see it, feel it, give it, and get it.

"

CARRY YOUR DIGNITY WITH A CROWN AND OWN IT.

- ACE

Dignity is a mirror of pride. You must posses this quality in order to excel in all areas of your life. Dignity must be carried like a jeweled crown, something that everyone can see, but cannot touch.

Protect your pride by remaining humble. This is another secret ingredient to success. Those who are successful know their dignity is everything that they are, and because of this, they protect it.

Wear your dignity like no other, and watch as people gravitate to your grandeur. Self worth is everything, and you must know that before anything else, your dignity is your gravity.

Let it keep you grounded so that it can lift you.

> POSSESS SO MUCH SELF ESTEEM THAT IT SHINES BRIGHT ENOUGH TO BLIND THOSE WHO COULDN'T SEE YOU BEFORE.

– ACE

If self esteem could were visible, it would resemble a roaring lion. Esteem for yourself is the ultimate supremacy. It defines your character as solid, definite, and confident.

Set your standards high, and make those around you rise to meet them. You may be afraid to shine, but owning your self esteem, is like holding a diamond, whether you want it to or not, it is going to shine.

Those who didn't recognize your greatness before, will have no choice but to see it, and acknowledge it for all that it is worth.

Blind them with the things you always possessed. Your light will never let you down.

> WITH FAVOR COMES FEAR. THOSE WHO FAVOR YOU MAY ALSO FEAR YOU.

– ACE

What I've learned is that the same people who love you can also hate you. The same people who honor you may be the same ones who want to see your demise.

This also means that the same people who favor you may be fearful of you. Your favor can attract people who want the same favor you have. They may envy your blessings and conceal their fear of you, by getting close to you.

Always be mindful of protecting your gifts. Your favor is your gift, remember that it belongs to you, it was created for you, because it was meant for you.

Be mindful of the people closest to you, they may also be the ones who fear you. You are in control at all times. Guard your gift.

> YOU CANNOT NEGLECT YOURSELF AND EXPECT OTHERS NOT TO DO THE SAME.

— ACE

Put yourself on a pedestal. Do not expect anyone else to love you the way you will love you. Be your own priority and watch how others prioritize you in return.

There is no better feeling than being valued for who you are within yourself, and watching others gravitate to you because of the love they see you giving yourself.

Never neglect the best parts of you. That includes your mind, body, spirit, and soul. No one can love something that does not nurture or love itself first.

Neglect does not yield nurturing. You must find your own way of expressing self love, and watch it come back to you time and time again.

> WALKING IN SELF ESTEEM ALLOWS YOU TO RUN INTO YOUR TRUTH, FREEDOM AND HAPPINESS.

– ACE

When you learn how to walk as a baby, it is challenging, it is awkward, and it is downright uneasy.

You may fall, stumble, and even bump into a few things in the process, but eventually you figure it out, and your ability to walk becomes second nature.

Walk so strong in your self-esteem that it comes as second nature to you. Do not allow others misery to dim your light in any shape, form, or fashion. What you possess, no one else can claim.

The moment you learn how to walk in your self-esteem, is the moment you learn how to run into your destiny, and fly into your purpose!

> SOMETIMES YOU HAVE TO GIVE YOURSELF A STANDING OVATION, EVEN WHEN THERE IS NO ONE ELSE IN THE CROWD.

— ACE

Many times in life you will find that some of the greatest moments of your life will not be captured, or you may have to experience them alone.

You will also find that you have to cheer for yourself even when there is no one in the crowd to cheer you on.

Always be your own cheerleader, learning to do this will allow you to appreciate the support you receive along the way from your true cheerleaders.

There is nothing like knowing that when you believe in you, others will too, and even if they don't, know that you are walking in the right direction regardless of anyone else's approval.

> THE TRUTH ABOUT RESPECT IS THAT IT WORKS FOR YOU EVEN WHEN YOU'RE NOT AROUND.

– ACE

Respect is a gift that keeps on giving. It is a machine that runs endlessly even when you are not directly operating it.

When you put respect out into the world, it becomes a virtue that pursues you endlessly. Respect is not just given, it is a principle that many people live by, and therefore it must be earned.

Always respect yourself, those around you, and those who came before you. The cycle of reverence has to be passed on and continued. Take the time to slow yourself down, honor the best parts of who you are.

Set your standards high, and continue to raise the bar. Respect yourself first and foremost.

Whether you are around or not, your name should be respected and associated with respect in the highest regard.

CHAPTER 4
SELF-APPROVAL is AFFIRMATION

> SELF APPROVAL IS THE GREEN LIGHT FOR BLESSINGS.

— ACE

Whether you are a faith based individual or not, it is important that you keep in mind one very key rule in life. That rule involves fully approving of yourself that will allow positive energy to flow into your life.

When you successfully locate a space in which you are happy with who you are, abundance will overflow into other areas of your life as well.
Be a portal of contentment within your deepest self, and dig deep to understand who you really are.

In doing so, you will unearth a new self of confidence, assurance, and certainty which will to a welcomed sense of secure in who you are.

Know that this process is one day at a time, and that the process itself never stops. Neither does your growth. Grow into approval of yourself and flourish.

> IT IS NOT UNTIL YOU APPROVE OF THE PERSON YOU ARE, THAT THE WORLD WILL APPROVE OF YOU AS WELL.

— ACE

How can anyone understand someone that doesn't understand themselves? They can't. The same goes for love, faith, trust, and self-worth. You must come to grips with the fact that who you are is who you are meant to be, and that will never change.

You were created to be exactly who you are on purpose! It is your ultimate responsibility to live with purpose ON purpose! Do not allow social media, peer pressure, or any other distraction detour you from working towards your goals.

Stay laser focused on being content with who you are so that the rest of the world, whether they approve or not, will know exactly who and what you are. A force.

> HOW CAN A BLANK CANVAS DISAPPROVE OF ITSELF. BE THE BLANK CANVAS NO ONE CAN DISLIKE, DISAPPROVE, OR DISMISS.

– ACE

When you look a white wall, the first thing you envision is painting it or decorating it. Before any type of ornamenting transpires, it is simply a blank canvas waiting to become whatever you want it to be. The same principle applies to your life.

Everyday that you wake up is a new day, a new chance, a new canvas for you to make out of it whatever you so desire. Your mind already knows what your heart wants to do, now you must go out and do it!

Be your own motivator. Be your own inspiration. Act on instinct, and follow your heart until your canvas becomes filled with color, images, and dreams that are attainable.

No other person can define who you want to be, and who you know you already are deep down inside.

"

WHEN YOU LIVE LIFE ON YOUR OWN TERMS, THERE ARE NO CONDITIONS.

- ACE

There are no terms and conditions that come packaged with you when you are born. You do not come with a set of instructions or a guide that tells people who you are, and how to treat you as you go through life. The same goes for your existence.

Do not put terms and conditions on your life that will inhibit you from being the person you truly want to be. This is called living in a box.

Step out of this box, and always remember this life is what you make it. No terms, no conditions, just whatever you want, need, and require.

>

PERMISSION IS FOR THE POWERLESS.

— ACE

When you are in a position of power, who do you need permission from? You must live in power, like any great leader in this world does.

Those in positions of power do not seek permission to be great. This is what makes them great. You have the power to do the same.

Live your life on your own terms, and without permission. Permission is for the powerless.

Be great and know that you don't need permission to do so.

> THE BIGGEST ENDORSEMENT YOU COULD EVER GET, IS THE ONE YOU GET FROM YOURSELF.

- ACE

Be your own billboard. When people see you, you must resonate a greatness that draws them towards you. You are your biggest cheerleader, and you are your biggest motivator at all times. This also applies to validation.

You are your greatest endorser. No one should ever have to endorse you, the way that you will. How can they? No one knows how great you are the way that you do. Let this shine through, and give off a radiance that attracts other greats to you.

Who you see in the mirror will always be the biggest, and best endorsement to yourself. That's you.

"

VALIDATION STARTS WITH YOU AND ENDS WITH YOU.

— ACE

Validation is the first cousin of permission, approval, and authentication. You are the only person that can dictate all of them. Validation is a form of confirmation that comes from you, starts with you, and ultimately ends with you.

You are not born to be validated by anyone but yourself. When you seek validation from others, you are also seeking approval, and happiness in places and people that cannot give it to you.

Happiness starts where you allow it to, and that is with you. No **VALIDATION** required.

"

EXPECTING APPROVAL, IS LIKE EXPECTING REJECTION. YOU HAVE TO KNOW THAT IT EXISTS, AND ACCEPT IT OR MOVE ON.

– ACE

Acceptance and rejection are one in the same, because they both come from others. When you live your life based on the acceptance or rejection of others, you will never truly find the answer you may be looking for.

Look within yourself, and the answers will naturally come to you. If you want to shave your hair and dye it blonde, or go out and get tattoos, or even if you want to learn a new language, do it because that is what your heart is telling you to do. Not because of anyone else's approval or rejection.

Take both with a grain of sugar, make it sweet, turn outcomes into what you want them to be, and move on in the best possible way.

"

WHEN YOU CAN ACCEPT YOURSELF AT YOUR WORST, EVERYONE WILL EMBRACE YOU AT YOUR BEST.

- ACE

Owning your flaws when you are at your lowest point is the first step in regaining your strength to rebuild. You can construct a life that no one else could ever imagine for you, because only you know what that life is.

When you are able to embrace the worst side of yourself, others will embrace the best side of you.

Be a lover of yourself at all times, through the good and the bad, and in the process others will love you throughout your journey, no matter where you are as well.

> YOU DON'T NEED PERMISSION TO BE WHO YOU ALREADY ARE!

— ACE

When you were born, you were born with the same traits that you still possess. The traits that make people love you, like you, or hate you.

No matter what, you never needed permission to be who you were born to be. Your life is what you make it, and that includes the permission to be whoever you so choose to be.

Always remember that you don't ever need permission to be who you already are!

CHAPTER 5
SELF-LOVE is APPRECIATION

> WHEN YOU UNDERSTAND THAT SELF LOVE IS THE BEST LOVE, YOU WILL FIND TRUE LOVE.

— ACE

Love starts with you. Take the time to get to know yourself. Take yourself on dates. Travel and venture out with yourself to new places. Fall deeply in love with yourself.

In the process you will find a new sense of worth and appreciation that you cannot find anywhere else. When you go out, you will attract a new type of energy towards you. People love people who know themselves.

When you understand that self love, is the best love, that is when you will find true love. True love understands all of the above. Love yourself, and love will come back to you in every way.

>

NO ONE WILL EVER UNDERSTAND YOU, NURTURE YOU, OR LOVE YOU THE WAY YOU WILL LOVE YOU.

– ACE

Loving yourself is the first and most important step in fulfilling your purpose. There is no one on this earth who will ever be able to understand you the way you will understand yourself.

There is no one in this world who will be able to nurture the parts of yourself that you can tend to and nurture. And there is no one on this planet who will ever love you the way you will love you.

When you decide to put yourself first, you will meet someone who will be willing to do the same. You will not be disappointed with the outcome of this approach. Self love is the best love.

"

LOVE COMES IN MANY FORMS, BUT YOU'LL ALWAYS KNOW THAT IT'S REAL LOVE WHEN YOU LEARN TO LOVE YOURSELF.

– ACE

Once you've learned to love yourself, you will know how to decipher love from others. If love is what you want, it will come to you when you least expect it.

Love gravitates to those who are loving. You must be the reflection of the thing you want to achieve and obtain. If love is a goal in your life, you must love yourself wholly, and fully, and truly, so that when you meet someone, they will know what standard of respect they must give you.

No matter what form love comes in, you will always know what it is, because you took the time to love yourself first.

> FIGHT FOR WHAT YOU LOVE UNTIL YOU DON'T HAVE TO FIGHT ANYMORE.

- ACE

The words fight and love are polar opposites. In a sense, they don't belong in the same sentence. The reason why they do make sense together is because you have to fight for the things that matter the most, for many people, love is one of those things.

You have to put a certain amount of effort into the things you want to obtain, love being a major part of our human lives.

When you show the person that you love, that you are willing to fight for their love, you will get the same in return. And if you don't get it in return from them, there will be someone else that comes along who will.

Always know that your efforts do not go in vain, and what is meant for you will be.

"

LOVE CAN CURE
YOU IN THE MOST
IMPOSSIBLE WAYS.

- ACE

Love is the strongest drug in the world. It is the most powerful antidote anyone can ever experience. Love is something that we thrive on.

Wherever you are in the world, you can find love. I believe that love finds us. It is a power that can bring the absolute best out of us. Love at its best is power. It is almost as necessary as food and water.

Every living thing in this world requires love to thrive. Whether love hurt you in the past, always know that it can cure you as well. It can cure you to the point that you forget about anything that happened before. Love heals all.

"

IF LOVE IS HURTING YOU, CONFUSING YOU, OR DISAPPOINTING YOU. IT'S NOT LOVE.

- ACE

Many people confuse love with something that is hurting them, confusing them, or disappointing them. The truth of the matter is that love is none of those things.

Love is accepting, nurturing, understanding, and comforting. Love is the very thing that can heal you from the wounds of your past, in such a way that you forget how you were ever hurt in the first place.

Do not allow something that is hurting you to tell you that it loves you. Where there is love, there is not pain. There may not always be pleasure, but someone that loves you will always comfort you.

> LOVED PEOPLE LOVE PEOPLE. DON'T ALLOW THE PAIN OF YOUR PAST TO STOP YOU FROM LOVING AND BEING LOVED.

— ACE

Hurt people hurt people. Loved people love people. Be the love you wish to receive. It is about taking the things and people that hurt you, and using that to rebuild your heart in such a way that love comes back to you ten fold.

You have to be open to receive the love you want. It is nothing worse than blocking your own blessings and love by being jaded from your past.

The past will never change, so allow it to better you wherever you are. Do not allow the pain of your past to stop you from loving and being loved.

"

BE YOUR OWN HERO
BEFORE YOU GO
TRYING TO SAVE
SOMEONE ELSE.

- ACE

Have you ever tried to save someone else while you were drowning? It would be impossible. The same goes for trying to put someone else before yourself in order to make them happy.

You have to first build the best version of yourself that you possibly can, and then at that point, you can go forward in being the help someone around you may need.

You cannot save anyone without making sure that you are secure first and foremost.

> LOVE IS THE MOST POWERFUL ANTIDOTE ON EARTH. LET IT GIVE YOU POWER AND PLEASURE NOT PAIN.

— ACE

Love is the most powerful thing on earth. Love has the power to change a nation. It can bridge gaps and bring people together from around the world.

Always keep in mind that love is power, and power must be used the right way. It is not meant to be taken advantage of, or abused.

Love is meant to give power, pleasure, and gratification, not pain. Tap into the best parts of love, and watch it work in your life. It will always work to bring the best you out of you.

> "

LOVE IS THE MOST POWERFUL ACTION IN THE WORLD. USE IT, DON'T ABUSE IT. NURTURE IT, DON'T NEGLECT IT.

– ACE

Love is something that is continuous. It is a deity that never dies, and has to be nurtured in order to work. The best feeling in the world is knowing that the people who love you can be trusted. You have to be utterly secure in these feelings.

When you understand how to water your garden of love, it will do nothing but sprout, grow, and flourish. It has no choice but to give you the same love you give it, over and over again.

Love is truly an action word. Nurture it for what it is meant to be used for, don't abuse it, and expect to get it back.

CHAPTER 6
SELF-TRUST is CERTAINTY

> TRUSTING YOURSELF IS LIKE FINDING REFUGE IN A STORM. KNOW THAT YOUR HEART AND YOUR INSTINCTS ARE A SAFE PLACE YOU CAN ALWAYS RELY ON WHEN ALL ELSE FAILS.

- ACE

Trusting your instinct is like knowing that when you eat a full plate of food, the food will make you content. It is a given in its most obvious form.

Self trust, is self peace. You have to know that you will not let yourself down, even when all else fails. Be the refuge you seek in a storm, and find comfort in your mind, body, and soul.

You cannot be a failure to yourself, when you are all that you have. When you learn how to be a safe place for yourself, you will become a safe place for others as well.

> SUCCESS IS NOT A MISTAKE. NEITHER IS WHERE LIFE TAKES YOU.

— ACE

None of the good things that happen to you are by mistake. Everything happens for a very distinct and concerted reason.

All the places that you go are meant to teach you a lesson. All of the people that you meet are meant to teach you something new, and bring the best out of you.

Life takes you where it is supposed to take you because it a part of your journey. Take all of the best moments and parts of your life, and use it to build a monument you can be proud of forever.

"

WHEN YOU GET TO A POINT IN YOUR LIFE WHEN YOU KNOW EXACTLY WHAT YOU WANT, THERE IS NOTHING THAT CAN STOP YOU.

- ACE

Knowing what you want is knowing yourself. Knowing yourself is confidence. When you wake up everyday, you have to know what your purpose is, and what you are living for.

What are you working towards everyday that you go out into the world, and make an impact? When you know who you are, and what you want, there is no one, and nothing that can stop you.

You become a force to be reckoned with, and that is power.

Live in that reverence, and always know that you are a machine meant to make an impact in this world.

"

THE ULTIMATE TRUST IS KNOWING THAT THERE IS ALWAYS MORE IN STORE FOR YOUR LIFE, WHETHER YOU CAN SEE IT OR NOT.

- ACE

Wherever you are in your life, you may have a sliver of doubt about what is yet to come. You are not meant to know what is in store for you.

You have to live every day to the fullest, and believe that the best part of your life is yet to come. Live in confidence that your life will turn out the way you want it to, if not better.

You could never imagine what is in store for, all you have to do is live, love, and believe.

"

WALK IN CERTAINTY THAT THINGS WILL GO IN YOUR FAVOR. AND TRUST THAT THE BEST PART OF YOUR LIFE IS HAPPENING.

- ACE

No matter what state your current life is in, you must believe that better things are in store. You must walk in certainty, knowing deep down inside of yourself that things will work out in your favor.

Just thinking positive thoughts will lead your life in the right direction. Be a firm advocate that no matter what, your turn will come. Your happiness is in progress.

More than likely, you are living the best part of your life, just by being alive. Live do not exist, and know that the best is yet to come.

"

EXPECT THE BEST,
RECEIVE THE BEST.
TRUST YOURSELF.
AND THE WORLD
WILL FOLLOW.

- ACE

You are a magnet of the things you believe. When you expect the best out of situations, you will receive the best out of them. When you trust yourself, people in your life will trust you.

When you become the reflection of what you see, you will begin to notice that the world is following your lead.

Be a leader of good habits, good virtues, and positive vibes. The world has no choice but to follow.

"

DISAPPOINTMENT IS A DIRECT RESULT OF DEPENDENCE ON SOMETHING YOU COULDN'T TRUST IN THE FIRST PLACE.

- ACE

We are only disappointed when we place our faith in something or someone that we couldn't depend on in the first place.

Many times, we are given red flags on the things that will disappoint us later on down the road. In fact, these things show us the flags themselves.

It is up to us to decide whether or not we are going to allow something or someone outside of ourselves to be an upset.

Depend on the things that you know will not disappoint you, and in this process you will build a fort of fulfillment. Dependence will disappoint you. Depend on yourself, and leave the heartbreak out of the equation.

> WE ALL POSSESS A SENSE OF HOPE THAT ONE DAY, WE WILL PROVE EVERYONE WHO DOUBTED US WRONG. THAT'S TRUST.

— ACE

It is so rewarding to prove to those who doubted you, that you can achieve success, love, and happiness with or without their approval.

Believe in the voice in your head that pushes you to go further, harder, and longer to achieve your goals and dreams. Your dreams belong to you for a reason. Act on them and don't look back to any seeds of doubt.

Allow the hope inside of you to exceed your expectations, and prove every little skeptic wrong. Always strive to prove yourself right. It's not about anyone else but you.

> ENTRUSTING MY LIFE IN SOMEONE ELSE'S HANDS WOULD REQUIRE TRUSTING MY SOUL WITH THEM AS WELL. NOTHING COMPARES TO THIS KIND OF CERTAINTY.

– ACE

When you find someone that you can trust, you have to embrace it.

Being able to trust anyone outside of yourself, is an honor and blessing to the soul. It is a feeling that cannot be described in words. It warms the heart knowing that you can put your faith, trust, and heart in the hands of another.

There is nothing that compares to fully trusting someone. This engraves a sense of certainty that when everything goes wrong, you can trust they will be there, ready to keep you assured.

> INVEST YOUR RELIANCE IN GUARANTEED RETURNS. BE THE SURENESS YOU WISH SOMEONE TO BE TO YOU.

– ACE

In order to get what you want, you must first be that very thing you are seeking.

Invest your time, love, and energy into the people that will give those things back to you. You will feel a sense of assuredness knowing that you are not wasting your most precious commodities.

Live with a sense of certainty and be willing to step out of your comfort zone in order to get what you most deserve.

Life has an amazing way of returning what we invest. Invest in those guaranteed endowments and you will always get them back.

CHAPTER 7
SELF-FREEDOM is
DECLARATION

> SELF FREEDOM IS LIKE HEAVEN ON EARTH. WHEN YOU CAN SET YOURSELF FREE, ANY AND EVERYTHING BECOMES POSSIBLE.

– ACE

Freedom is peace. Freedom is liberty, and everything that is free. Living your life in this way allows you to be more receiving and understanding of you truly are, and what you wish to give back to the world.

You can set yourself free at any point you so wish to, and when you do, you will find your best self yet.

Being free is like Heaven on earth. It is a way of life, that no one can place you in other than yourself. When you set yourself free, everything you've ever considered becomes possible.

> FREEDOM IS A FEELING EVERYONE DESERVES TO FEEL IN THEIR LIFETIME. IT IS OUR RIGHT TO BE FREE IN ALL THAT WE DO.

– ACE

Freedom is a right that we are all entitled to while we are alive on this earth. No matter what type of life you lead, you deserve to live it in freedom.

As we go through the motions of life, we choose to conform, and that is where unhappiness stems from. It is our God given right to be free in all that we do, whether personally or professionally, you make the choice to wake up and go out after what you believe the most in.

Live in this freedom and watch as your water falls over the greatest parts of your life.

"

BREAK YOUR HEART FREE. BREAK YOUR SPIRIT FREE. BREAK YOUR MIND FREE. AND BREAK YOUR SOUL FREE. WHEN ALL OF THIS IS DONE, ALL OF YOU WILL BE FREE.

- ACE

Freedom is a process. It begins with you making the decision to be free. Once your mind is made up, you must allow your heart, body, and soul to follow.

The choice to be free is the most liberating feeling you will ever experience amongst feeling true love, and being able to trust.

When you break free of being bounded by society, you will grow to learn that freedom to be who you want to be was always yours.

You must learn who, what, and where you want to be in order to embrace freedom, and the liberation that comes with it.

> THE WAY BIRDS FLY, IS THE WAY YOU DESERVE TO LIVE. YOU MUST SET YOURSELF FREE IN ORDER TO FLY.

— ACE

The flight of a soaring bird is the most intriguing sight to see. The freedom birds experience from flying, is the same freedom we as humans strive for when we wake up and go for our dreams.

Achieving our dreams is the moment we fly. We must first decide that we want to be free in all that we do. Nothing is stopping you, or holding you back, unless you allow it to.

You can take flight at any moment of your life that you so choose to. It is ultimately up to you to go out and free yourself. Be as a free as the flight of a soaring bird, and take your happiness along the flight with you. You will never regret it.

"

FREEDOM IS YOUR CHOICE. IT IS A PERSONAL AND MENTAL DECISION. WHEN YOU DECIDE TO BE FREE IN ALL ASPECTS OF YOUR LIFE, YOU DECIDE TO LIVE THE BEST LIFE DESTINED FOR YOU.

- ACE

There is no better feeling in the world than being free. Making the decision to be free also means that you are making a decision to live in your happiness.

Being free can mean a number of different things to different people, but it is ultimately up to you to decide where you see yourself being happy.

It may be you coming to your family to express your feelings for the same sex, or it may be taking a new career path in a different part of the world, or enrolling in culinary school.

Whatever your happy place is, find it, because this is the same place you will find your independence.

> LIVING IN LIBERTY IS THE ONLY WAY TO LIVE.

– ACE

This would be an entirely different world if everyone lived in liberty. If there were no rules, no laws, and no authoritative orders. People would be more willing to operate on their own terms. Live this way now.

Stop allowing others to dictate your freedom and liberties in the life that you were given on this earth.

Be so liberated that it inspires others to do the same. As humans, we tend to gravitate to well-known people, often times because they are very care free in their lives.

They do not harbor in others opinions. This is the same principle I urge those around me to operate in. Living in liberty is the only way to live.

"

THE BEST MOMENTS
IN LIFE ARE THE
ONES THAT WE ARE
FREE IN.

- ACE

Our technology driven world often drives us to forget to live in the moment. We are consumed by the lives of others as we try to keep up with the millions of unrealistic images that we see online and in the media.

We want to capture everything we do for the gratification and approval of others, when in fact we should be living to satisfy ourselves. When we return to what matters, and what feeds us, we find out how great life really is.

Be spontaneous more often, do the unexpected more often, smile more often, and do good deeds more often. Each of us will come to find that life without parameters is the best life you can live.

> FREEDOM IS WHAT WE LIVE FOR. IT IS THE DREAM THAT WE CAN MAKE REALITY. IT IS THE UNINHIBITED PART OF OURSELVES THAT LIVES INSIDE OF US UNTIL WE DECIDE TO SET IT FREE.

– ACE

All of the dreams that we see, come to us because they are things that we can make reality.

Subconsciously, we place a hold on ourselves by doubting the images that flash into our minds. signals for us to go out and make happen. You can only live when you decide to set yourself free.

You will never be able to make your dreams a reality unless you inhibit yourself. Act on the things that once held you back, and go for everything that belongs to you. Uncage the power inside of you, and live like nobody's watching.

> LIVE. BE WILD AND FREE WITH THE COLORS YOU CHOOSE. AND FRAME IT FOR THE WORLD TO SEE.

— ACE

Going into an art museum is one of the most intriguing experiences you could EXPERIENCE. Art has the power to make your mind wander into a space within yourself that you never knew existed.

We must adopt this same the life that you live everyday. Know that you have ultimate authority to go out and paint the wildest, most vivid colors of your heart... the colors you choose to paint your life with must come from what makes you most happy.

Whether it be love, food, travel, music, family, friends, or all of the above, it is up to you to use these colors to paint a reflection of who and what you are. When your masterpiece is complete, frame it for the world to see.

"

THE BEAUTIFUL THING ABOUT FREEDOM, IS THAT IT BELONGS TO YOU WHENEVER YOU WANT IT WITHOUT LIMITS OR RESTRICTIONS.

- ACE

Being free is a gift that will always give; not only to you, but also to others. Freedom is a commodity that is dependent solely on you. You must decide that you want it, and then take it when you are ready.

The most beautiful aspect of freedom is that it is free. Being free is an honor, because it tells the higher powers that be, that you are willing to accept the beauty created for you to see.

There is beauty inside of yourself and in those that come into your life. There are no limits, no restrictions, and no constraints on your life when you make the choice to be free. Start now, and don't look back!

"

THE BEAUTIFUL THING ABOUT FREEDOM, IS THAT IT BELONGS TO YOU WHENEVER YOU WANT IT WITHOUT LIMITS OR RESTRICTIONS.

- ACE

Being free is a gift that will always give; not only to you, but also to others. Freedom is a commodity that is dependent solely on you. You must decide that you want it, and then take it when you are ready.

The most beautiful aspect of freedom is that it is free. Being free is an honor, because it tells the higher powers that be, that you are willing to accept the beauty created for you to see.

There is beauty inside of yourself and in those that come into your life. There are no limits, no restrictions, and no constraints on your life when you make the choice to be free. Start now, and don't look back!

ABOUT THE AUTHOR

Amber Chaisson is an American author, vocalist, and songwriter who lives in Atlanta, Georgia.

Amber was born in Homestead, Florida and grew up as an Air Force brat and has lived in more than 10 different cities of the United States. Amber left Dallas, TX to pursue a professional music career in Atlanta, Georgia and in the process found her voice in writing inspirational books.

Her inspirational social media content caught the attention of a well-known publicist which led to her first published book. Amber's days are spent in the studio recording music and writing for major artists.

When not in writing mode, Amber enjoys designing clothes for her clothing line, cooking and working out. As a community advocate, Amber also enjoys volunteering and speaking to youth at schools.

To learn more about Amber and her upcoming projects, follow her on social media @theamberaffect or visit

WWW.THEAMBERAFFECT.COM.

www.ingramcontent.com/pod-product-compliance
Lightning Source LLC
Chambersburg PA
CBHW070619300426
44113CB00010B/1588